The Little Book

of

Civil War Reenacting

An introduction for those who want to try it out

William J Watson, editor
www.wmjwatson.com
ISBN-13: 978-0615450209 (Broken Lance Enterprises)
ISBN-10: 0615450202

So you think you want to try out this Civil War reenacting thing, huh?

Great!

Let's see if we can't help you get started in a really good way. Those of us involved are universally enthusiastic about it.

Those folks you saw at the parade or the museum or the battlefield look pretty interesting in their old timey clothes, whether military or civilian. Some of that stuff looks pretty elaborate. And how do they find the time to learn the drill and the craft of camping using Civil War equipment and technology?

Hey, guess what? We use manuals written for the soldiers of the Civil War for the military stuff. They've been called "drill manuals written by geniuses for use by idiots," which is us for sure. But that's just the beginning. The drill and the camps are all out in the open. But what you see is like an iceberg – 90 percent of it is below the surface. And if you can't see it, you can't know whether it matters. It does. That's why we wrote this book. ("We." My name is on it. I had lots of help from other folks who want to see all the people whose interest in this period of time is renewed by the 150th anniversary of the events get involved in a useful, intelligent and enjoyable way.)

Here's a quick "Frequently Asked Questions" to help you decide if you want to do this and if so, what to expect. (One of the mantras of the savvy, happy Civil War reenactor is to manage your expectations. You'll find out why later on.)

Skits for the public are usually a big hit at living history events

Is it expensive?

Yes – and no. If you want to get into it in a serious way, it has some costs that are, at first glance, pretty stiff. If you want to try this out to see if you like it, it will cost you very little. Why? Because any unit worth joining – and you will, in all likelihood, become part of a reenacting club – has clothing and gear to loan people who want to try it on for size. It might not all fit perfectly, but guess what? That's authentic. Our joke is that Civil War uniforms came in three sizes: Too big, too small, doesn't fit. We'll go into actual costs if you read on and decide, "Yes, I'll try it out."

Is it time-consuming?

Yes – and no. If you get addicted, it can become your life. It almost always involves long weekends: Travel on Friday, event attendance Saturday and Sunday, travel home Sunday night. Sometimes travel on Friday means taking the day off work. And travel on Sunday means getting home late. On the other hand, getting you ready to try out an event will take about an hour, including an intense lesson on weapon safety and enough drill to keep you from hurting yourself. Or anyone else.

Are there a lot of reenactors?

What's a lot? The real answer is "nobody knows." In 1998 "we" had heavy attendance at the 135th anniversary of Gettysburg. We had 24,000 reenactors present, and we had about the same number of men in Pickett's Charge as the original. (We believe the Confederates sent about 13,000 men across the field.) That may have been the highest attendance ever at a Civil War event, and we're pretty sure it wasn't all the reenactors available. Some folks had other obligations.

However, everyone involved seriously in the hobby agrees our numbers have declined. At the start of the Civil War Sesquicentennial, there were perhaps about 20,000 United States citizens involved, scattered across the country. Civil War Campaigner magazine lists 35,000 or so readers around the world. People from other countries travel to the United States for events, but American Civil War events are also held in England, Germany and France, as well. It's one of the reasons travel is a factor in the hobby: Very often a lot of people have to travel a long way to make a battle have the numbers and feel as epic as history demands.

Explaining children's toys to the public

Is this a family activity?

Yes – and no. If you are interested in seriously pursuing recreating history as accurately as possible, then opportunities for full family involvement are more limited. If you are more interested in weekends where only part of the time is spent in "Civil War mode" and the rest of the time is spent in relatively modern socializing and logistical support, you'll have more opportunities to deploy the whole family. But not the dog. Civil War events are horse-friendly, but not, generally, dog-friendly.

I get the feeling there are differences in how people approach this hobby. Am I right?

Oh, heck yes. Yes, indeed. While it is difficult for anyone involved in the hobby to be dispassionate and disinterested when describing these differences, we'll give it a try.

Everyone is in this for the fun and fulfillment of the

Photo courtesy of Bob Ward

experience. What that experience is, however, varies, as does "your mileage" for what fun and fulfillment mean.

Some prefer as much historical activity as possible, starting with their arrival on site and continuing unbroken until they pack up their gear to leave. That means 1860s food, 1860s and earlier technology, a full agenda of 1860s activities for the weekend, etc.

Some prefer battles and drills as the focus and limit of their historical activity, with the rest of the weekend spent eating modern food, etc.

The amount of historical activity vs modern logistical support and modern activity varies across that range. Each event is different.

Individual events cater primarily to a given part of the reenacting spectrum. Obviously, someone who wants to be issued a slab of bacon and a potato is not going to get that at an event where everyone else brings a camp kitchen, complete with a gas ring and modern food. Conversely someone showing up at a historically intense event with a gas ring is not going to feel at home.

These things are, at the event level, usually made clear in advance, so it shouldn't become an issue for you. That's the "manage your expectations" part of all this. Know what to expect and if an event doesn't seem like one you'd enjoy, you've got a choice: You can simply not go, or you can go with eyes wide open as to what you'll find.

A great many folks adjust their expectations, their equipment and their behavior and attend events that are not to their preference, just to be able to spend a weekend reenacting rather than mowing the lawn, taking out the garbage, and couch potatoing.

With such a relatively small number of reenactors – 20,000 in a nation of 240 million people – how does everyone even stay in contact?

Hey, it's the age of the Web, Facebook and e-mail. Like a lot of niche interests, Civil War reenactors increasingly are using digital technology to overcome geographic dispersal. There are online forums where reenactors gather to share thoughts, ideas, and opinions. And almost every Civil War event held now has its own Web site, complete with information to "manage expectations" and ways to register online.

Why do reenactors reenact?

There's no one single reason. Some people like to act, to become something they aren't. Others enjoy experiencing history. Some are deploying that part of the genetic code that says "Humans will find fulfillment working in small groups to achieve a goal." Others are paying tribute to their ancestors who were in the war, or to those people in the war even if they weren't relatives. For some it's simply a vacation away from the 21st Century, a change of pace. Still others enjoy figuring out how people of that time

History on the march: Confederates at Port Republic, Va.

Federals in heavy marching order, Port Republic, Va.

made themselves happy and comfortable under difficult conditions. (It turns out our ancestors were pretty clever folks.) There are still others who deliberately seek to use their leadership skills as part of their own personal development, and in some cases people discovered they actually had leadership ability even though they weren't looking for it.

Who are you people?

History geeks is the latest term to pop up, although it is not universally cherished as a self image. Living historians is the dignified term. Experimental archaeologists pops up sometimes.

Reenactors come from just about every walk of life. We have mechanics, carpenters, salesmen, lawyers, elected officials up to the level of state Senator, clergy, doctors, firefighters, ranchers, farmers, butchers, bakers, and at least six candle-stick makers. We have active and non-active military. (Some reenactors who left to go on active duty in Iraq and Afghanistan immediately resumed reenacting when they got home.) We have "former ranks" from private to colonel. It is fun watching a former real colonel, now a reenacting private, taking 1862 orders from a former real private now a reenacting lieutenant. Actually, for some, that's the point: Whatever you are in the modern world, you are something else in the 1860s, and the change has its own appeal for a lot of people.

Is there a national organization?

No. Apparently the gene for personal independence that empowers many of us to put on funny clothes, drill with obsolete weapons and engage in an activity many people find incomprehensible has secondary effects. One of those is a strong dislike for imposed conformity. This is over-generalizing, but: You can more easily show a reenactor why a particular uniform is better than another with reason than you can make him wear it with a rule handed down by a national organization. History geeks, yes; but collectively we seem to be most like a herd of cats. And the largest organizational unit for cats is, for a pleasing play on words, a pride. Used in another way, an appeal to pride is a fairly consistent motivator for reenactors, to do what they do to the best of their ability.

You may be saying "but a national organization doesn't have to impose unwanted standards, it could be a fun thing." Yup, keep talking, sooner or later that will occur to enough people. Meanwhile, we slog forward without that.

If there's no national organization, how are you organized?

By hobby clubs, associations of clubs called "umbrella groups," and by events.

The smallest "unit" is three to six people who travel together, reenact together, eat together, and share duties and experiences. It's hobby name is a "mess," based on Civil War word usage describing the same-size group that did those things, although they of course were not reenacting.

Next up is a more formal group, usually with more people, with elected officers, meetings, and all the things that go with any club. It can be six to about 70 people, and the members often try to depict a

Massed and masked Confederates awaiting the 8th NYVI at Pence's Farm

particular regiment or artillery organization or cavalry regiment about which they have specialized knowledge. (Most will set that "unit impression" aside if it is too glaringly inappropriate for a particular event.)

In the United States right now, several larger organizations exist, consisting of two or more separate reenacting clubs allied to create battalions with more historically realistic numbers. Arrangements vary, but typically two to six clubs can put up enough people to consistently create a 30-member company, and three to five companies is considered enough to create a reasonable facsimile of a real regiment or battalion. The larger organizations have varying standards for member clubs, including event attendance, impression standards, safety and good behavior. They are known collectively as "umbrella organizations." Some of the larger ones, with membership from more than one state, include the Mifflin Guard (http://www.mifflinguard.org); the National Regiment (http://www.nationalregiment.com); the US Volunteers (www.usvolunteers.com); and Army of Northern Virginia (http://bonnieblue.net). Some smaller organizations: The Palmetto Battalion (http://www.palmettobattalion.org), a statewide organization at the heart of secession in South Carolina; the 2d New Jersey Brigade (http://www.2dnjbrigade.org) a statewide New Jersey outfit with samples of civilian, medical, and military components. There's also Pridgeon's Shenandoah Legion (http://www.pridgeonslegion.com/) and the Southern Division (http://www.southerndivision.org) for mostly Confederate impressions with a lot of "operational," that is, 24/7 "on duty" operations. Federals looking for the same thing can start with the Potomac Legion (http://pl.mainecav.org/) and the Third Regiment of the United States Volunteers (http://www.usvolunteers.org/usvmainpage.html). These all have their own Web sites, and a search online by name will turn them up. (We list their links, but URLs can change occasionally, so if the link seems dead, use your favorite search engine.) There are many, many more organizations, with either more or less emphasis on historical purity in their philosophy. Ask questions. Find one that fits what you want to do. Most will help you find a unit based geographically in your area.

There are folks who have attempted to list every reenacting club out there on Web sites. http://www.civilwarhome.com is one; be advised the "groupings by state" means the state "impression" the club does. The Twelfth Alabama, for instance, might actually be in Delaware. Here's another site (http://nps-vip.net/history/reenact/index.htm), which is regularly updated.

Not all clubs belong to umbrella organizations. Some "fall in" with other independent clubs at bigger events to create an ad hoc regiment. Others maintain cordial but informal relations with one or more umbrella groups so they can fall in as guests.

At the event level, organizers select overall commanders for Union and Confederate forces. They in turn invite various umbrella groups and open registration to anyone willing to meet the event standards and rules. Reenacting events are organized around identified battles. The goal is usually to recreate, plausibly, some aspect of a particular battle or campaign.

Still interested? OK.

What's the first step?

Find some reenactors. Contact them. Introduce yourself. Express your interest. Ask questions about the things they do, the events they attend, the goals they set for themselves.

You'll find reenactors several ways.

Many communities have Memorial Day parades, both north and south – yes, northerners, there is a Confederate Memorial Day in some states – and often Civil War reenactors are prominently in the parade. The Civil War, after all, is what gave sad birth to Memorial Day. Go talk to them. Before the parade, while they are forming up in the staging area, might be the best time. After the parade they are liable to be winded or

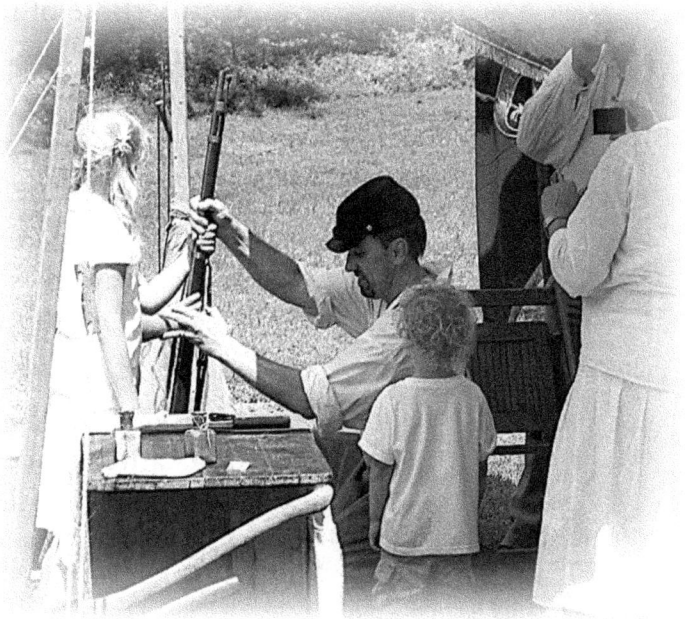

Civil War reenactors can often be found at museum living histories explaining the past to the present

eager to get to whatever is next. During form-up, someone will be there an hour early. It's a good time to talk.

You can also find them by looking online, using search engines or the links in the last section.

There are also online forums where reenactors and those interested in reenacting can interact. One of the most venerable (www.cwreenactors.com) is run by Bob Szabo, an expert in taking photographs using Civil War-era equipment and techniques. The site also includes reference material, lists of places to buy gear, and a search engine so you can perhaps find a previous discussion on a topic you're interested in. The site is intended, in part, for newcomers to first search the site for information and then, if there are still question marks, ask questions in the various forums dealing with civilian and military reenacting.

Ultimately, this isn't a hobby done on the cheap. Suppliers of equipment and clothing rise to the level of a cottage industry and that's all; there is no Wal-Mart for uniforms. Even the roughest and most inaccurate uniforms cost a chunk, and the weapons are expensive. If you get hooked on this, it will probably cost you about $2,000 to get completely, properly outfitted. That is still, those of us addicted to the hobby will tell you, less than it costs for a bass boat, a season of NASCAR attendance, or good clubs and greens fees for golfing.

The ultimate cost would include a firearm, trousers, shirt, suspenders, coat, socks, drawers, shoes, hat, canteen, haversack, cartridge box, belt, bayonet, scabbard and cap box, plus basic mess gear: fork, spoon, tin cup, maybe a metal plate or a canteen half for a plate. Then you need a rubber blanket, wool blanket, and at the minimum a shelter half – half a dog tent – or a wedge tent. Prices for these items change over time, although they never seem to come down.

Cavalry reenactors face higher costs. As one pointed out, it's not the saddle, leather, horse, trailer or horsefeed that's the killer, it's buying the farm. Again, if you already have a horse, others will cheerfully help you try it out with the right saddles and bridles and whatnot.

You'll spend a lot of time answering questions after you load up on information

There is, also, the issue of quality. Some vendors selling merchandise for the hobby are not selling anything a soldier from 1862 would recognize. Cheaply made uniforms of heavy blanket wool are not only wrong, they're often not good for you. The correct material costs more, last longer, and, most importantly, works better. It does not stifle you in the summer heat of Gettysburg or Vicksburg. It keeps you warm in the Shenandoah Valley in April. It is that way for every single item. The closer to the original you can get it, the more authentic and comfortable you're going to be. And, of course, it costs more than a knock-off made in Pakistan. The up side is that it holds its value better. If you are changing impressions or have a career change that makes reenacting impossible, items made by quality vendors can be resold relatively quickly.

Remember, you don't have to spend all that much to get started. A stable, active, outgoing reenacting club will have loaner gear so you can try it out.

Where do I learn what's expected of me?

First and foremost, from history. There is no substitute for knowledge. One of the attractions of reenacting for many participants is the

Musicians drill at a living history on the Gettysburg battlefield. Reenactments - opposing fire - are not permitted at national battlefield parks. Living histories are permitted.

joy of learning more and more and more about a time, a place, a unit or a person. For purposes of getting started, though, you'll find yourself taking guidance from whatever unit (hobby club) you join or fall in with, and from the rules and "impression" guidelines for each event.

Most units have standards for uniforms and equipment and safety and activities. Some have them written out, with others they are implicit.

Most events have event regulations. They are usually not overly elaborate, except in some extremely history-heavy smaller events where expectations for authenticity are very high. But they do set your expectations for an event. We've included some samples. Here's a couple of caveats:

• Weapon safety will be required at any event you want to attend, which means you need to have clean, functional, safe weapons before you leave home. If you borrow a weapon, it is still "on you" to make sure it isn't loaded when you take it, and that it is clean and functional and safe.

• Rules on alcohol are common, and usually they say "no alcohol." This is not universally enforced except when someone goes too far and creates a problem. On the other hand, even at events where alcohol is permitted, that's AFTER the battle, not before. And in the other direction, if it's a state or national battlefield, when they say "no alcohol" they mean "no alcohol," and they have no sense of humor at all. It's not because they get a thrill by enforcing rules. It's because they are safeguarding ground consecrated by blood.

Here's a possible epiphany: You can drink whenever you want. You can only do Civil War reenacting once in a while. Seize the moment.

A sample of event rules.

"At High Tide," a three-day event that recreated several specific regiment-on-regiment fights from the battle of Gettysburg, was held on private ground outside Gettysburg within the past decade. It drew several thousand reenactors and was one of a growing number of events put on by reenactors for reenactors (rather than by historic venues or by commercial interests trying to create a tourist attraction or simply turn a (big) profit off the reenactment itself). What follows was donated to this project by Chris Anders, a lifelong reenactor and a primary event organizer for this and other Mid-Atlantic Civil War events.

AT HIGH TIDE

The following rules are in place to insure maximum authenticity and enjoyment for all participants, and also to be sure we properly represent history to the public. The spectators who attend reenactments today are far more educated than in the past, so it is our responsibility to them to raise our standards so as not to disappoint or mislead them. All questions concerning these regulations should be addressed to the event host. Thank you for your participation.

There will be four main camps. Two will be military only camps for the respective sides that will be run as military camps of 1863, period. There will be an authentic civilian camp that will have specific authenticity regulations and limited participation. There will also be a "camp of convenience" for those who wish to camp mixed (civilian and military together) which will be separate from the military camps, and have their own logistical support and camp chain of command.

These rules apply to all participants equally.

1. No illegal drugs. THIS IS A ZERO TOLERANCE POLICY.
2. Artillery and cavalry by invitation only.
3. No specialty impressions (Lee, Grant, Lincoln, Davis, female soldiers,

vivandiers, foreign observers, general's without commands, Belle Boyd, Indians, zouaves -unless specifically called for in a scenario), seaman, marines and so forth- are allowed without pre event approval. Please contact the event organizer with any questions concerning this.

4.   There will be 4 main camps established- the First two will be military only camps for the respective sides that will be run as military camps of 1863, period. Next there will be an authentic civilian camp that will have specific authenticity regulations and limited participation, and finally a camp of convenience for those who wish to camp mixed (civilian and military together) which will be separate from the military camps, and have their own logistical support and Camp Chain of Command.

5.   No excessive drinking will be permitted in any camp, period.

6.   Military: All commanders will be held liable for the actions of their troops, both on and off the field.

7.   Civilians: There will be a civilian coordinator on site, and all are encouraged to work together to improve their experience. Any Civilians wanting to enter the Military camps must receive a pass to do so.

8.   ALL participants must be in period dress from 7 a.m. Saturday through Sunday after the battle. Anyone not attired in period dress will be asked to leave the period camps.

9.   No modern items are to be open to public view. Camps will be patrolled by the provost to insure maximum authenticity at all times.

10. No cars will be allowed in camp after 11 p.m. Friday until after the battle on Sunday. No participants are allowed to break camp prior to the Sunday battle.

11. No dead animal parts on uniform or weapons. This means plumes, feathers, animal tails or other such ornamentation, unless prior documentation is provided to the event organizer.

12. No Zouave muskets, Kentucky rifles, shotguns, Hawken rifles, or any other weapon not of the 1863 timeframe will be allowed without prior approval and documentation.

13. NO modern glasses, shoes, watches or any other clothing item will be allowed. This is a zero tolerance policy. ZERO.

14. All military impressions should be of the 1863 period. See the "Looking 1863"portion of the web site.

15. Children in the camp of convenience must be dressed as per children of the 1860's, not as kids in uniforms playing war with cap guns...this will not be allowed.

16. Correct Corps Badges required for the Federals as dictated by the scenarios.

17. Only commissioned officers will be allowed to carry side-arms, with the exception of mounted troops who will be allowed one pistol per person.

18. Only full-scale artillery allowed. This means 57" inch wheels. We are limiting the number of guns per side to allow for more historical portrayals. Please contact the organizers prior to registering as Artillery.

19. No unscripted hand-to-hand combat will be allowed.

20. All troops not following orders from the respective commanders will be

asked to leave the event.

21. Each camp will be patrolled by event staff to insure maximum authenticity at all times. No modern food containers, coolers or beverage containers will be allowed out in public view. All companies and participants that require the above conveniences must keep them hidden at all times during public hours and are strongly encouraged to do so at other times. This is to increase the quality of the event for reenactors and spectators alike. If a company violates this policy they will be subject to be removed from the event at the discretion of the staff.

22. No participants under the age of 16 will be allowed to carry weapons at any time, on or off the field.

23. All participants under the age of 16 must be functional musicians to be allowed on the field and no one under the age of 13 allowed on the field at all. This is for both authenticity and safety reasons.

24. Ramrods are not to be used at any time during the battle

25. Those participants who portray barefooted soldiers are permitted to do so, however, the event is in no way responsible for injuries caused by this portrayal.

26. All troops are encouraged to carry a full kit during the battles - blanket or knapsack, as the troops involved in this battle had just covered long distances during the campaign, and would have outdistanced their supply wagons.

27. Any horse on site must be listed on your registration form.

(Note that the rules reference other guidance, specifically something called "looking 1863." It is additional material to help reenactors fine-tune their "impression." We've included it here:)

Federals Looking 1863

One aspect of the hobby that will increase both your knowledge and enjoyment of an event is tailoring your impression to the specific event. This allows you to learn more about the material culture as well as giving the public a better vision of the troops of the period.

This is the event for the "uniform soiled" look. With the majority of uniforms and gear now being issued by the National Government combined with the hard campaigning seen by these boys, a dusty and worn out look to your kits is encouraged.

In order to illustrate the items, I have original photos of these items with the description. Be sure to view them carefully, and I have found if you look at them for a minute or two, do something else, and them go back, you will see details that normal viewing does not pick up.

Keep in mind these suggestions only cover the period from Mid June to late July, 1863, and are not intended for other periods.

Head Gear

There are three basic choices for this period. For most units the standard federal forage cap is the rule, however some units, such as the Iron Brigade, were wearing dress hats, and some like New York state troops were wearing state-issued kepis.

Some photographic evidence exists of many units wearing civilian hats, but be sure to document this to the unit or units you are portraying for the weekend.

Havelocks were not worn at this time of the war.

CORPS BADGES MUST BE CORRECT FOR THE UNITS YOU ARE POR-TRAYING!

Coat

There are several options for this as well. The most common would be the standard US issue fatigue blouse, made out of 8-ounce wool flannel and lined. There are many photographs of field adaptations to these garments, from adding additional buttons to pockets, both inside and out.

US Issue dress coat (Frock). These were worn heavily during this period, and especially for units such as the Iron Brigade.

Trousers

During this period the Standard Issue Foot Trousers in Sky Blue Kersey would be the most prevalent.

Footwear

US issue Brogans would have been most common, with private purchase boots also represented.

Canteen

This is the event for the leather sling or canvas sling. Smooth side with a jean or blanket cover. Only the first canteens ordered had the sky blue cover, the rest were either of sack coat lining (jean, flannel) or out of US issue Blankets. Take a look at the color photo of surviving sack coats and the various hues to see what color the canteen lining may have been.

Knapsack

Most units would have been carrying the US pattern double bag knapsack, although many units may have been using blanket rolls, both the short and long roll.

Shirts

Federal-issue flannel shirts would have been the most common seen, with state issue and civilian shirts also acceptable.

Confederates Looking 1863

One aspect of the hobby that will increase both your knowledge and enjoyment of an event, is tailoring your impression to the specific event. This allows you to learn more about the material culture as well as giving the public a better vision of the troops of the period.

The common Confederate during this campaign traveled light and looked hard. They still would have been covered in road dust, and since the central government was now in charge of supplying the men, the look was far more uniform than seen previous.

Keep in mind the clothing a North Carolina soldier wore during this period may or may not have differed from that which a Virginia private wore. Some individual states did equip many a regiment, such as North Carolina, but there is no hard rule that says if you are from North Carolina you would have been wearing a North Carolina jacket. But it is a detail grossly under represented in our hobby.

In order to illustrate the items, I have original photos of these items with the description, as well as Weaver's account of how he determined the "rebel" dead from the "national" dead when he was hired to rebury only the Federals in the New National Cemetery. This perhaps is the best view of the CS soldier during this campaign.

Head Gear
There are many choices, and your decision would be based upon what unit you are depicting.
Choices could be-
Jean Cloth Kepi of gray or brown. You can see good examples of these in the Confederate Version of Echoes of Glory. Havelocks were not worn by this period.
Properly blocked and lined civilian hats, with little or no decorations or hat brass.

Coat
There are several options for this as well.
Richmond Type II is the preferred coat. This is a 7-9 button jean or satinette short jacket, with epaulets, some having belt loops as well. This were mostly lined in osnaberg, with either block I or Federal general service buttons. Light gray was the most common color seen, with various undertones of brown, blue and green.
Other coats seen during this campaign, and thus as options are
North Carolina jeancloth shell jacket, Georgia shell jacket, South Carolina frock coats and civilian frock or sack coats.

Trousers
As with coats there are a few variations you could wear. Basic Richmond or civilian trousers should be the majority of trousers seen, with no trim on the seams.
These were sometimes lined 8 inches up from the bottom, allowing the

trouser to fall naturally over a pair of boots. These should be made out of jean or satinette, with some broadcloth and kersey trousers seen in the ranks. THIS DOES NOT MEAN FEDERAL ISSUE TROUSERS. This is a reenactorism, and highly overdone in the hobby. The fact is the CS Government did issue some sky blue trousers, but these were of their pattern, and not the federal government's.

Footwear
At this point in the War, Confederate or civilian shoes would prove to be the most common. The number of federal shoes worn by Confederate troops has been highly over estimated.

Canteen/Knapsack/Haversacks

This is one other area in which you can "appear 1863"
Most veteran troops would have confiscated U.S. smooth-side canteens and tarred haversacks. However, the common plain tin drum, with cloth or leather strap, would have been seen with newer units, as well as the common white confederate-issue haversacks.

In Fremantle's accounts, the bedroll was far favored over knapsacks, but a few units differed, and the occasional double bag would have been seen, as well as some English imported bags

(END of AT HIGH TIDE material)

Note that even these fairly detailed documents reference other documents, and photos, provided by the event organizer as a guide. You get the idea. A good event – and this one was a howling success – provides you with the information you need.

There's a footnote you'll probably appreciate to all this: While the list of clothing and equipment might seem daunting and discouraging, *most attendees had to do very little to "fit" the rules*. What's spelled out is essentially the "default" gear most reenactors have. What's ruled out is the oddball stuff that makes units look like fantasy armies rather than 186x military units. It makes a huge difference in the effect created, but it's your first encounter with the idea that "less is more."

What are events like?

There are several types of activities under the giant umbrella of reenacting.

Here's a description of a typical mid-Atlantic reenactment of 1,000 to 5,000 reenactors. The first section deals with military.

You arrive on site sometime Friday, check in at registration, and find your unit. You then unpack your gear, set up whatever camp you are going to have, and park your car in the designated area. There are probably camp chores necessary: firewood for cooking, water for canteens and cooking, helping others with their tentage or shelter. Friday is a good night for going down to "sutler row," the shopping mall in tents for clothing and gear that springs up like a crop of mushrooms at these events, to pick up some needed item. On Friday it often takes a long time for the camp to quiet down, as people who haven't seen each other for weeks or months socialize.

Saturday morning, history takes over, with the various

Canteen detail can take up a lot of time

units in their battalions awakened by bugle, drum and fife. First thing up is morning roll call, where the company first sergeants line everyone up and take roll. It is historically authentic. It is also the first actual hard information on how many are present, of what ranks. At events that strive for maximum realism, the morning rolls are used to decide what weight of issued rations to distribute. At almost all events, the morning rolls are sent up to battalion headquarters so the battalion officers know how many muskets they have.

There's usually a few minutes to tidy up the sleeping areas – many units want the company streets to look like a period military bivouac

The Potomac Legion drills on the Gettysburg National Battlefield Park, near the First Minnesota monument

or fixed camp, not a fraternity house or youth hostel or skid row. Then, depending on your company and battalion officers, you may have breakfast, or you may have company drill first. Either way, expect a company drill in the morning and probably a battalion drill before noon as well. Very often battalion drill will involve using some of the maneuvers expected to be used during battle, which often will be sometime in the afternoon.

Crowds of spectators will throng the area – just as you did before you accepted the blue or grey coat – and at some point the armies will fall in, form up, step off, and a battle of greater or lesser realism will take place.

Very often when the battle is over company first sergeants will, after the "dead and wounded" have had a chance to find the company again, call the roll to make sure no one is "really" missing. There may be a march to camp, or the company or battalion may be released at the post-battle mustering site so members can pursue their own individual desires. "Off duty" is probably a good way to think of this time.

Then dinner, then an early sack time – usually everyone is tired Saturday night – and you get up again Sunday and do it all again.

There are variations. Some events go "operational" Friday night, and you can expect to find yourself pulling picket duty for two hours. These events usually feature more ground and, sometimes, less rigid formulas for battles. You may be part of a patrol. You may be in a skirmish line trying to develop the enemy's position. Your company may be designated to "support" a battery of guns – positioned to protect them from enemy infantry. You may have officers concerned with selecting bivouacs from which you can be deployed in a hurry, officers concerned with things like defilade, marching speed, defenses against cavalry, etc. You may find yourself changing location on Saturday, stacking arms when you halt and throwing down your bedding near the arms stacks (it is a fast and foolproof way to form a battalion in less than five minutes: You 'fall in' on your arms stack, and the battalion is formed.

At some events you and your company may find yourself asked to interact with spectators, either in planned demonstrations or as they walk through the camps. You would be expected to be giving them accurate information as best you can and saying you don't know when you don't know. A lot of people are hungry for information about history, especially when you're eating salt pork on a hardtack cracker after cooking it all up on a canteen half over an open fire. A lot of folks find it simply amazing. A lot of folks have wrong information about history. (That includes some reenactors, but we're working on it.)

If you opt for cavalry, you can expect to spend quite a bit of your time looking after your horse. Just about every cavalry reenacting unit has a hard core of "horse people who reenact" who set high standards for care of the beasties.

If you opt for artillery, you can expect to spend quite a bit of your

You get your picture taken a lot. Potomac Legion bivouac east of the Pennsylvania Monument, Gettysburg National Battlefield Park, living history

time looking after the gun and getting safe drill hammered into your head. Just about every artillery reenacting unit has a hard core of dedicated artillery fanatics who are quite aware that there are many ways to get serious hurt around something that shoots a half-pound of powder with each shot, even without projectiles. The guns are just another kind of beastie.

That's a reenactment. A great many reenacting clubs do their own "living histories" at national battlefield parks, state battlefield parks, public and private museums, country fairs, history venues, community festivals and, also, after parades, especially Memorial Day. Living histories usually involve setting up a model camp and conducting firing, cooking, and drill demonstrations, with or without a formal schedule, and spending a great deal of time interacting one-on-one with spectators. Sometimes it requires a lot of energy and a lot of organization. Big crowds can really keep you on your feet and talking. This is often the place, however, where units pick up new recruits, so it serves several goals.

"Graces" is an 1800s children's game in which two sticks that look a lot like knitting needles are used to toss a hoop that looks suspiciously like an embroidery hoop.

Civilians

Yes, there are opportunities for civilians, including children, at most events. There are both civilian-only reenacting organizations and other "clubs" that include both a military and civilian component. You can find out more about the different styles or intensities among civilian reenactors from the same sources listed for soldiering. And here's a great link from a civilian reenactor who went to the trouble to assemble a list of primarily civilian groups:

http://www.geocities.com/txcwcivilian/other_groups.html

Female soldiers?

Editor's note: "Women in the ranks" are forbidden some clubs and by some events, while others don't even care if women are wearing makeup and necklaces while carrying a musket. The middle ground appears to be women can and do actually look and act like a man while in uniform. We have the resident expert on that, Audrey Scanlan-Teller, with some tough-love advice on how to do it in a historical context.

Among the millions of soldiers who fought in the Civil War, current research suggests that from eight hundred to perhaps several thousand women disguised themselves as men to enlist in the Union and Confederate armies and serve as soldiers. Although women were forbidden by army regulations to enter military service in both the Union and Confederate armies, four women soldiers left written accounts documenting their service, while many others were revealed when accident, sickness, wounding or capture made others aware of their true gender. These discoveries were so astonishing to their peers that they are recorded in army paperwork, in the letters and diaries of surgeons, nurses, and other soldiers, and others were reported in contemporary newspaper accounts.

Women soldiers often served undiscovered in the ranks for several years. Some went undetected throughout their enlistment term and returned to civilian life following the war. Others died from wounds or disease taking their secret with them to the grave.

How was this possible?

First, some regimental surgeons conducted very cursory exams at the soldier's enlistment. One woman soldier, Sarah Edmonds, wrote that the only thing the surgeon looked at when

"Albert Cashier" was really Jenny Hodgers, a private in Company G, 95th Illinois Volunteer Infantry. Her gender wasn't discovered until she was badly hurt in an accident 50 years after the war and required surgery.

she enlisted with the 2nd Michigan Infantry Regiment was her hands!

Second, the soldier's uniform was very effective at hiding the gender of the wearer. Thanks to Victorian social ideals and distinct gender roles, nobody expected a woman to wear pants or, more startling yet, be a soldier.

Furthermore, the demographics of the ranks including many young men and boys with scant facial hair and higher-pitched voices helped young women to blend in.

A woman who wants to reenact as a soldier has a difficult task. Today's ranks of reenactors generally are older than those of the original cast, with people in their forties and fifties being the norm, rather than their mid-twenties. Women stand out more with this age group than they would have surrounded by ranks of younger men. The biggest hurdle is overcoming the fact that we Americans are used to seeing women wearing pants, shirts, jackets, and ties. The clothes do not make the man as markedly as they did in the 19th century.

However, there are things that a woman can do to help her male disguise:

Cut the hair to a short length or if longer hair is a must, make certain it is tightly twisted up and or braided on the top of the head and kept secured out of sight under the hat. A forage cap works best for tucked-up hair.   No loose ponytails; that is so 18th century.

Do wear loose fitting clothing. When it is appropriate to the unit's impression, longer sack coats or frock coats help hide a woman's wider hips. Looser fitting trousers also help hide hips.

Suspenders can help hide a narrower waist and wider hips and flatten the line of the chest as well, but they do make answering the call of nature a bit more time consuming.

Wearing a binder will flatten and secure a woman's chest from the hits it can take in a battle reenactment. The instructions to make a binder can be found here: http://web.archive.org/web/20050220091031/www.geocities.com/womansoldier/guidelines1.html

Do not wear make-up, earrings, nail polish, or pretty pink ribbons as a hat band. If a woman does not want to be mistaken for a man during an event, she should not take on a soldier's role.

Because a woman is supposed to be hidden among the men, she

should expect to behave as one of the boys. The camp environment can resemble a men's locker room at times. Run with it.

As a military reenactor, a woman should expect to do whatever duties are assigned the other soldiers and pitch in as needed.

Women who portray soldiers can get extra scrutiny at reenactments. For certain events, a woman may need to submit a photograph of her soldier's impression upon registering. Some events will ask a woman soldier to leave the event if she can be identified as being a woman. Some events ban women entirely. The key is having an impression so good, that like the original cast of women soldiers, the men do not know the beardless youth among them, is, in fact, a woman. *-AS-T*

The end or the beginning?
It's up to you. There's your introduction. Here's some inspiration:

The Eighth New York Volunteer Infantry gets ready to go up an open hill and into the waiting muskets of Trimble's massed and masked brigade, shown in an earlier photo. The reenactment is on the original spot of the fighting on Widow Pence's Farm, part of the battle of Cross Keys in Virginia. "History heavy" reenactors from more than a dozen organizations banded together 200 strong to create the Eighth as part of a preservation to raise funds and awareness of the development threat to Cross Keys and Port Republic battlefields.

This pamphlet is provided to you by:

The contact information for this organization is:

Produced for the Civil War community
by Broken Lance Enterprises,
home of "Books Guys Will Read",
http://www.wmjwatson.com
featuring history-heavy fiction. The site also has additional resources for reenactors
and potential reenactors.

Electronic versions of this pamphlet are available free online at smashwords.com;
look for "The Little Book of Civil War Reenacting." Feel free to reproduce the print
version, also. Spread the word! Reenacting is fun!

If you found this book useful, you may be interested in "Seize the (Reenacting) Day!",
a guide for reenactors who want more history in and from their reenacting experi-
ences.   http://www.wmjwatson.com/p/books.html

www.ingramcontent.com/pod-product-compliance
Lightning Source LLC
Chambersburg PA
CBHW080537030426
42337CB00023B/4771